The Taunton Press

Published by
Jo Sharp Pty Ltd
A. C. N. 056 596 439
P.O. Box 357 Albany 6330
Western Australia
©1999, All rights reserved
Printed in Australia

The Taunton Press, Inc.
63 South Main Street
P.O. Box 5506
Newtown, CT 06470-5506
www.taunton.com
email: tp@taunton.com

Taunton
BOOKS & VIDEOS
for fellow enthusiasts

Distributed by Publishers Group West

ISBN 1-56158-364-2

Acknowledgments

Creative Director *Jo Sharp*
Garment Design *Jo Sharp, Leanne Prouse, Coby Yzerman, Lucia Russo.*
Knitting *Norma Beard, Sonia Charewicz, Wanda Chudzik, Margaret Cusick, Janice Darrah, Lily De Roost, Francesca Greaves, Jenny Green, Betty Hawkins, Hazel Heggie, Gwen Howson, Sheila Min, Connie O'Brien, Leanne Prouse, Whitney Weaver, Coby Yzerman.*
Photography *Jo Sharp, Andrew Markovs, Rita Markovs, Lisa Thompson.*
Photoraphy Styling & Assistants *Bronia Richards, Leanne Prouse*
Models *Cindy Dean, Ruth Wernham, Gavin Mehrtens, Suzie Dickson*
Hair *Hot Lox Salon, Albany*
Make Up *Chrisy Byrne*
Accessories *Sussans, Albany*
Hand Woven Wrap *Designed & crafted by Nessie Cruse using Jo Sharp Yarn*
Carpets *Carpet World, Albany*
Location credits *Rookleys Cafe, Albany, Spice Island Furniture, Albany.*
Film Processing *Rainbow Pro Photo Lab*
Book Design *Stumpfel Shaw, Bronia Richards, Jo Sharp*
Knitting Graphs *Stitch Painter Gold*
Computer Consultant *Scott Parsons*
Colour Separation and Prepress *Multicolor Australia*
Printing *Frank Daniels Pty Ltd, Western Australia*

CONTENTS

alt	alternate
approx.	approximately
beg	beginning
cm	centimetre
col	Colour
cont	continue
cn	Cable needle
dec	decrease
dia	diameter
foll	follow/ing/s
inc	increase
incl.	inclusive
k	knit
K1B	insert needle through centre of st below next st on needle and knit this in the usual way, slipping the st. above off the needle at the same time
Kb1	knit into back of next st.
M1	make one - pick up loop between sts and K into back of it
mm	millimetre
p	purl
patt	pattern

KNITTING BAZAAR

Precious Ariel

My Paragon

My Boheme and I

A kaleidoscope of colour

Serendipity

Jewels to wear

Shining from the

Brunswick Boulevarde

A thoroughly

Metropolitan emporium

Gaze upon a safron sunrise

A Darjeeling hacienda

Where we have stayed

My Ebony, my Georgia

My Avalon and I.

TENSION

At the start of each pattern, the required tension is
given. Before you begin knitting the garment, it is
most important that you knit a tension square. Usi
the stitch and needles specified in pattern, cast on
sts and knit approx. 40 rows. Lay work flat and
without stretching, measure 10cm both vertically a
horizontally with a ruler. Mark with pins. Count t
stitches and rows in between the pins, these should
match the required tension. If not, you will need t
change your needle size. Smaller needles will bring
the stitches closer together, larger needles will spre
the work out. Incorrect tension will result in a mis-
shapen garment.

SIZING

Sizes ranging between S, M ,L, XL are given for ad
garments, while children's sizes are given by age.
Unisex sizing is rated A, B, C, D. It is advised, whe
knitting unisex sizes for men to use sleeve size D .
The bodice circumference measurements given in
each pattern are calculated after a 2cm seam
allowance has been deducted. Bodice diagram
measurements have no seam allowance deducted.
Sleeve measurements are taken from underarm
whereas diagram shows full sleeve length. To
ascertain which size garment to knit, use as a guide,
favourite old sweater which fits the intended wearer
well. Compare the measurements of this garment wi
the measurements given in the pattern diagram and
knit the size which most closely matches the existin
garment. Note that some patterns are designed to fi
snugly, whilst others are loose fitting. Each pattern
accompanied by a photograph and in most cases, fo
adult patterns, the garment modelled is the medium
size.

YARN QUANTITIES

Quantities of yarn are based on average requirement
using specified tension and Jo Sharp 8ply DK Pure
Wool Hand Knitting Yarn. Responsibility cannot be
accepted for finished garment if substitute yarns are
used.

ARIEL

Knitting Rating: Beginner with Intarsia Knowledge.

MEASUREMENTS

Women's Sizes	S	(M	L	XL)	
To fit bust	80	90	100	110	cm
Bodice circumference	110	118	128	136	cm
Bodice length	62	62	62	62	cm
Sleeve length	40	40	40	40	cm

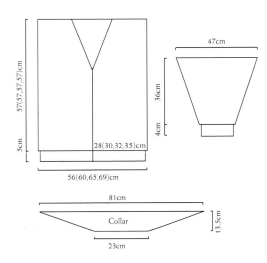

NEEDLES

1 pair 3.75mm (UK 9) (USA 5)
1 pair 4.00mm (UK 8) (USA 6)

BUTTONS

Version 1 - 4 x 3.5 x 2.2cm (N42 Durango Buttons)
Version 2 - 4 x 2.5 x 1.7cm oval shaped.
See page 107 for details on Durango Buttons.

YARN

Jo Sharp 8 ply DK Pure Wool Hand Knitting Yarn.

No.	Key	Colour	Yarn Quantity				
Sizes			S	(M	L	XL)	
Version 1							
Col 1	☐	Smoke 339	14	14	15	15	x 50g balls
Col 2	▣	Owl 801	2	2	2	3	x 50g balls
	✦	Terracotta 332	1	1	1	1	x 50g ball
	◣	Aegean 504	1	1	1	1	x 50g ball
	✚	Ruby 326	1	1	1	1	x 50g ball
	·	Antique 323	1	1	1	1	x 50g ball
	✕	Mosaic 336	1	1	1	1	x 50g ball
	■	Lilac 324	1	1	1	1	x 50g ball
	❖	Antique 323	yarn allocated above				

Ariel Version 1, left

Contued on page 13.

Version 2

In this version, simplified motifs will later be embroidered.
See below for embroidery shades.

No.	Key	Colour	Yarn Quantity				
Sizes			S	(M	L	XL)	
Col 1	☐	Jade 316	11	11	12	12	x 50g balls
Col 2	▣	Embers 804	3	3	3	3	x 50g balls
	✦	Embers 804	yarn allocated above				
	◣	Terracotta 332	1	1	1	1	x 50g ball
	✚	Terracotta 332	yarn allocated above				
	·	Jade 316	yarn allocated above				
	✕	Embers 804	yarn allocated above				
	■	Embers 804	yarn allocated above				
	❖	Embers 804	yarn allocated above				

Version 2 Embroidery					
Gold 320	1	1	1	1	x 50g ball
Brick 333	1	1	1	1	x 50g ball
Renaissance 312	1	1	1	1	x 50g ball
Cape 508	1	1	1	1	x 50g ball
Heron 802	1	1	1	1	x 50g ball
Slate 328	1	1	1	1	x 50g ball

TENSION

22.5 sts and 30 rows to 10cm measured over Stocking stitch and Intarsia using 4.00mm needles.

MOSS & RIB PATTERN

Row 1 (RS) *k3, p1, k1, p1 rep from * to end.
Row 2 P1, *k1, p5 rep from * to last 5sts, k1, p4.

BACK

Using 3.75mm needles and col 2, cast on 126(136,146,156)sts.
Work in Moss & Rib Pattern as follows;
Row 1 (RS) K0(2,1,0), *k3, p1, k1, p1 rep from * 21(22,24,26)times, k0(2,1,0).
Row 2 K0(2,1,0), p1, *k1, p5 rep from * 21(22,24,26)times, k1, p4, k0(2,1,0).
Change to col 1 and rep rows 1 & 2 until band measures 5cm ending with a WS row.
Change to 4.00mm needles and using st st beg with a k row refer to graph for col changes ** work 172 rows. Cast off.

LEFT FRONT

Using 3.75mm needles and Col 2, cast on 63(68,73,78)sts.
Work in Moss & Rib Pattern as follows;
Row 1 (RS) K3(2,1,0), *k3, p1, k1, p1 rep from * 10(11,12,13)times.
Row 2 P1, *k1, p5 rep from * 10(11,12,13)times, k1, p4, k3(2,1,0).
Change to col 1 and rep rows 1 & 2 until band measures 5cm ending with a WS row. Change to 4.00mm needles and using st st beg with a k row refer to graph for col changes **. Work 100 rows.

Contued on page 13.

BOHEME

BOHEME

Knitting Rating: Experienced.

MEASUREMENTS

Women's Sizes	S	(M	L	XL)	
To fit bust	80	90	100	110	cm
Bodice circumference	90	100	110	120	cm
Bodice length	46	46	46	46	cm
Sleeve length	48	48	48	48	cm

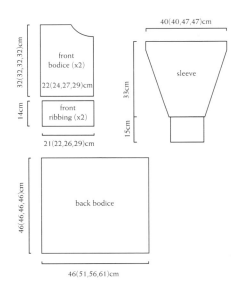

YARN

Jo Sharp 8 ply DK Pure Wool Hand Knitting Yarn.

Key	Colour		Yarn Quantity			
Sizes		S	(M	L	XL)	
Version 1						
Col A	Black 302	1	1	2	2	x 50 g balls
Col B	Embers 804	1	1	1	1	x 50 g ball
Col C	Brick 333	1	1	1	1	x 50 g ball
Col D	Mulberry 325	13	13	14	14	x 50 g balls
Col E	Ginger 322	1	1	1	1	x 50 g ball
Version 2						
Col A	Ink 901	1	1	2	2	x 50 g balls
Col B	Ruby 326	1	1	1	1	x 50 g ball
Col C	Forest 318	1	1	1	1	x 50 g ball
Col D	Navy 327	13	13	14	14	x 50 g balls
Col E	Violet 319	1	1	1	1	x 50 g ball

NEEDLES

1 pair 3.25mm (USA 3) (UK 10)
1 pair 3.75mm (USA 5) (UK 9)
1 pair 4.00mm (USA 6) (UK 8)
Stitch Holder

BUTTONS

Version 1 - 7 x 2.3 cm diameter
Version 2 - 7 x 3 cm oval (H48 Durango Buttons)
See page 107 for details on Durango Buttons.

Boheme Version 1

TENSION

Texture Pattern; 25.5 stitches and 42 rows measured over 10 cm using 3.25 mm needles.
Rib for Back; 36 stitches and 31 rows measured over 10cm using 3.75mm needles.

TEXTURE PATTERN

To make Bobble Insert needle into next st and cast on 1 st, then cast on a further 2 sts, k4 (the cast on sts plus the next st) pass the 3rd of these sts (2nd st from the tip of right hand needle) over the last st, then pass the 2nd and 1st sts, one at a time, over last st.

MOSS STITCH

Row 1 *K1, p1, rep from * to end.
Row 2 K all the p sts and p all the k sts as they face you. Repeat row 2 throughout.

COLOUR AND STITCH SEQUENCE

Note: Rows 5 - 8, carry yarn on WS of work.
Row 1 - 4 Col A, knit.
Row 5 K2 Col A, k2 Col B, rep to end of row.
Row 6 Knit Col A sts with Col A, and Col B sts with Col B.
(eg; K2 col A, bring col A to front, take col B to back, k2 col B etc)
Row 7 Knit Col A sts with Col B and Col B sts with Col A.
Row 8 As row 6.
Row 9 Col A, knit.
Row 10 - 11 Col C, knit.
Row 12 Col C, Moss st.
Row 13 - 14 Col D, Moss st.
Row 15 Col C, Moss st.
Row 16 Col C, purl.
Row 17 Col D, purl.
Row 18 - 19 Col D, knit.
Row 20 Col D, purl.
Row 21 Col D, k3, Col E bobble, rep to end of row. Carry yarn for bobbles at back of work.
Row 22 Col D, purl.
Repeat rows 1 - 22.

BACK

Using 3.25mm needles and col D, cast on
166(184,202,220)sts.
Row 1 *K4, p2 rep from * to last k4 sts.
Row 2 *P4, k2 rep from * to last p4 sts.
Rows 1 and 2 set patt for rib.
Work in Rib pattern as set, until work measures 8cm.
Change to 3.75mm needles and cont in rib until total
length measures 46 cm.
Cast off (RS) Cast off and AT THE SAME TIME
work the sts as follows; k4, * k3tog, k3, rep from * to
end. *(This method of casting off creates a firm edge for sewing
together)*.

FRONT RIBS

Left Rib Using 3.25mm needles and Col D, cast on
76(82,94,106)sts and work in rib as for Back until
work measures 8cm. Change to 3.75mm needles and
cont until work measures 14cm. Cast off as for Back.
Right Rib Work as for left rib.

LEFT FRONT BODICE

(knitted sideways starting at centre front opening)
Using 3.25mm needles and Col D, cast on
60(60,56,56)sts. Work rows 17 - 22 of Texture
Pattern, then work rows 1 to 22 of Texture Pattern.
Repeat rows 1 - 22 throughout.
AT THE SAME TIME **Shape Neck** Keeping Texture
Pattern correct, work 6(6,7,7)rows then inc 1 st at
neck edge of next row then every 6(6,7,7)th row
twice, then every alt row 5(5,6,6) times, then every
row 8(8,11,11) times.
Cast on 7 sts at beg of next row.
Work 54(64,70,80)rows straight *(omitting bobbles if they
occur less than 6 rows from last row to avoid bulky join on
seam)*. Cast off loosely and evenly.

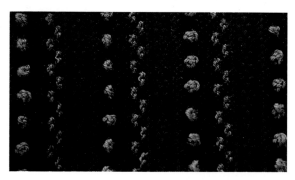

RIGHT FRONT

Make Right Front to match Left Front reversing all
shaping and working bobbles to align with Left Front
bobbles.

SLEEVES

Using 3.75mm needles and Col D, cast on
58(58,64,64)sts. Work in rib as for Back until rib
measures 6cm.
Change to 4.00mm needles and cont in rib as set until
rib measures 15cm in all, increasing 12 sts on last RS
row [70(70,76,76)sts].
Shape Sleeve Working in Reverse Stocking Stitch,
(ie work in stocking stitch beginning with a knit row on WS)
inc 1 st at each end of every 8(8,5,5)th row
10(10,15,15)times [90(90,106,106)sts]
[80(80,75,75)rows]. Work 18(18,23,23)rows straight
(adjust length here if desired). Cast off loosely and evenly.

MAKING UP

Join Front Ribs to Front Bodice pieces using Edge to
Edge stitch. Using Backstitch, join shoulder seams.
Centre sleeves and join. Join side and sleeve seams.
Button Band With Rs facing, using 3.25mm needles
and Col D, cast on 7 sts. Work in Garter st *(knit every
row)* until band, when slightly stretched, is the same
length as the Front bodice to beg of neck shaping.
Sew band into position as you work. Leave these 7
sts on a stitch holder at neckline. Mark position on
band for 7 buttons, the first to be positioned 2cm
from lower edge, the last to be positioned at top of
band, the other 5 spaced evenly between.
Button Hold Band Work to correspond with Button
Band, working 7 button holes opposite markers as
follows; k2, cast off 3, k2.
On next row, cast on 3 sts in place of those cast off
on previous row. Leave these 7sts on stitch holder.
Neckband and Collar With RS facing, using
3.25mm needles and Col D, pick up 7 sts from stitch
holder, 31 sts up right front neck,44 sts across Back
neck, 31 sts down Left Front neck and 7 sts from
stitch holder at left front neck [120 sts]. Work 6cm
in k2, p2 rib, keeping 7stitches of Garter Stitch
border correct, as follows;
Row 1 K9 * p2, k2, rep from * to last 7 sts, k7.
Row 2 K7 * p2, k2, rep from * to last 9 sts, p2, k7.
Change to 3.75mm needles and cont as set until work
measures 9cm. Cast off.

Boheme Version 1

BOULEVARD

BOULEVARD

Knitting Rating: Beginner Knitter.

MEASUREMENTS

Unisex Sizing	A	(B	C	D)	
To fit chest/bust	85	95	105	115	cm
Bodice circumference	98	112	118	132	cm
Bodice length	65	65	65	65	cm
Sleeve length	44	44	49	49	cm

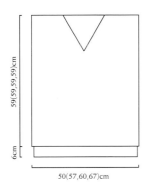

YARN

Jo Sharp 8 ply DK Pure Wool Hand Knitting Yarn

No.	Colour	Yarn Quantity				
Sizes		A	(B	C	D)	
Version 1 (Men's Sweater)						
Col 1	Antique 323	12	12	13	13	x 50g balls
Col 2	Hull 705	7	8	8	9	x 50g balls
Version 2 (Men's Sweater)						
Col 1	Khaki 329	12	12	13	13	x 50g balls
Col 2	Ebony 902	7	8	8	9	x 50g balls
Version 3 (Women's Sweater)						
Col 1	Embers 804	11	11	12	12	x 50g balls
Col 2	Heron 802	7	8	8	8	x 50g balls

NEEDLES

1 pair 3.25mm (USA 3) (UK 10)
1 pair 4.00mm (USA 6) (UK 8)
4 Double Pointed 3.25mm needles (USA 3) (UK 10)
4 Double Pointed 3.75mm needles (USA 5) (UK 9)

TENSION

22.5 sts and 33 rows measured over 10cm of Texture Rib pattern using 4.00mm needles.

Boulevard Version 1, left.

Boulevard Version 2, previous page, left.

Boulevard Version 3, previous page, right.

TEXTURE RIB PATTERN

Row 1 P2, K6 rep to end.
Row 2 Purl.
Rep rows 1 and 2, 3 times.
Row 9 & 10 Purl.
Rows 1 to 10 form pattern repeat.

STRIPE COLOUR SEQUENCE

Col 1, 5 rows
Col 2, 8 rows
Col 1, 2 rows
Col 2, 2 rows
Col 1, 3 rows
These 20 rows, repeated, form stripe pattern.

BACK

Using 3.25mm needles and Col 1, cast on 112(128,136,152)sts. Work in k2, p2 rib until work measures 6cm ending on a WS row.
Change to 4.00mm needles and working in Texture Rib & Stripe Colour Patterns together, work *185(185,186,186)rows *(adjust length here if desired)*.
Shape shoulders Cast off 9(11,12,14)sts at beg of next 6 rows, then 11(13,13,15)sts at beg of next 2 rows, then leave rem 36(36,38,38)sts on a holder.

FRONT

Work as for back to *. Work 124(124,118,118)rows *(adjust length here if desired)*.
Shape V Neck (RS) Purl 56(64,68,76)sts, turn, leave rem 56(64,68,76)sts on holder. Cont on these sts, dec 1 st at neck edge of next alt row, then every foll 3rd row 9 times, then every foll 4th row 7(7,8,8)times [39(,47,50,58)sts].
Work 4(4,7,7)rows straight [185(185,186,186)rows].
Shape shoulders Cast off 9(11,12,14)sts at beg of next row, then every alt row 2 times. Knit 1 row.
Cast off rem 11(13,13,15)sts.
Rejoin yarn to rem sts and complete second side to match first side, rev all shaping.

SLEEVES

It is advised, when knitting this unisex garment for a man, to use the size "D" sleeve.
Using 3.25mm needles and col 1, cast on 62(62,70,70)sts. Work k2, p2 rib until work measures 6cm, inc 12 sts evenly across last WS row [74(74,82,82)sts].
Change to 4.00mm needles and working in Stitch Patt as for back shape sides by inc 1 st at each end of 8(8,11,11)th row, then every foll 3rd(3rd,2nd,2nd)row 8 times, then every foll 4(4,5,5)th row 18 times [104(104,117,117)rows], [128(128,136,136)sts].
Work 23(23,26,26)rows straight, *(adjust length here if desired)*. Cast off loosely.

MAKING UP

Press all pieces, except ribbing, gently on WS using a warm iron over a damp cloth. Using Backstitch join shoulder seams. Centre sleeves and join. Join side and sleeve seams using Edge to Edge stitch on ribs.

Collar With RS facing, using 4, 3.25mm double pointed needles and col 1, pick up 62(62,68,68)sts along right side neck, 36(36,38,38)sts from stitch holder at back neck and 62(62,68,68)sts along left side neck [160(160,174,174)sts].

Working in k2, p2 rib, work 17 rows.

Change to 3.75mm needles and cont in rib for 152(152,166,166)sts, slip rem 8 sts onto 3.75mm needle, turn leave 8 sts unworked, slip 1 st, rib 143(143,157,157)sts, turn leave 8 sts unworked, slip 1 st, rib 134(134,148,148)sts, turn leave 16 sts unworked, slip 1 st, rib 125(125,139,139)sts, turn leave 16 sts unworked, slip 1 st, rib 116(116,130,130)sts, turn leave 24 sts unworked, slip 1 st, rib 107(107,121,121)sts, turn leave 24 sts unworked, slip 1 st, rib 98(98,112,112)sts, turn, leave 32 sts unworked, slip 1 st, rib 89(89,103,103)sts, turn, leave 32 sts unworked, slip 1 st, rib 80(80,94,94)sts, turn, leave 40 sts unworked, slip 1 st, rib 71(71,85,85)sts, turn, leave 40 sts unworked, slip 1 st, rib 62(62,76,76)sts, turn, leave 48 sts unworked, slip 1 st, rib 53(53,67,67)sts, turn, leave 48 sts unworked, slip 1 st, rib 44(44,58,58)sts.

Rep until 48 sts are left unworked each side, then rib to end of next row (including the 48 sts previously left unworked). Change to col 2 rib 2 rows (including the rem unworked 48 sts). Change to col 1, rib 2 rows, cast off in rib.

Boulevard Version 3, right

BRUNSWICK

BRUNSWICK

Knitting Rating: Average

MEASUREMENTS

Unisex Sizing	A	(B	C	D)	
To fit chest /bust	90	100	110	120	cm
Finished Bodice width	110	120	130	140	cm
Bodice length	70	70	70	70	cm
Sleeve length	41	41	48	48	cm

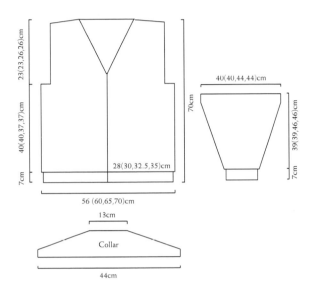

YARN

Jo Sharp 8ply DK Pure Wool Hand Knitting Yarn

Colour			Yarn Quantity	
Sizes	A	(B	C	D)

Version 1 (Men's Cardigan)

Owl 801	19	20	20	21	x 50g balls

Version 2 (Women's Cardigan)

Navy 327	18	19	19	20	x 50g balls

NEEDLES

1 pair 3.75mm (USA 5)(UK 9)
1 pair 4.00mm (USA 6)(UK 8)

BUTTONS

6 x 2.3cm dia.

TENSION

Measured over 10cm using 4.00mm needles.
Stocking Stitch; 22.5 sts and 30 rows
Herringbone Texture; 26sts and 36 rows

Brunswick Version 1, previous page right.
Brunswick Version 2, left & previous page left.

LEFT FRONT

Using 3.75mm needles cast on 63(68,73,78)sts.
Work in K2, P2 rib for 7cm. **Change to 4.00mm
needles and using st st beg with a k row, work a
further 35(35,32,32)cm ending on a RS row.
Make Garter Stitch ridge (WS) Next 2 rows; knit,
next 3 rows; purl.
Refer to Graph for texture patt and work rows 1 - 11.
Now repeat rows 8 - 11 until bodice measures
47(47,44,44)cm inclusive of band and ending with a
WS row**.
Shape Armhole (RS) Cast off 12sts, keeping patt
correct, knit to end of row and work a further
9(9,19,19)rows straight on these [51(56,61,66)sts].
Shape Neck Keeping patt correct, dec 1 st at neck
edge of every 4th row, 16 times [35(40,45,50)sts].
Shape shoulders Keeping patt correct, cast off
11(13,15,16)sts at beg of next and foll alt row. Work
1 row. Cast off rem 13(14,15,18)sts.

RIGHT FRONT

Work as for Left Front rev all shaping.

BACK

Using 3.75mm needles cast on 126(136,146,156)sts,
work in k2, p2 rib for 7cm , inc 1 st in last WS row
[127(137,147,157)sts].
Work rows as for back from ** to ** .
Shape Armholes Cast off 12 sts at beg of next two
rows, keeping patt correct, knit both rows to end.
Cont in patt on these [103(113,123,133)sts] until
back bodice length matches front bodice length,
incorporating shoulder shaping on last 7 rows thus;
Shape shoulders Keeping texture patt correct, cast
off 11(13,15,16)sts at beg of next 4(4,4,4)rows, then
13(14,15,18)sts, at beg of next 2(2,2,2)rows.
Cast off rem 33 sts.

SLEEVES

Using 3.75mm needles, cast on 54(54,62,62)sts.
Work k2, p2 rib for 7cm inc 12 sts on last (WS) row
[66(66,74,74)sts].
Change to 4.00mm needles and shape sleeve AT THE
SAME TIME working Row Sequence.
Shape Sleeve Inc 1 st at each end of every
6(6,8,8)th row 10 times [86(86,94,94)sts]
[60(60,80,80)rows] then every 5(5,6,6)th row 10
times [106(106,114,114)sts] [110(110,140,140)rows].
Work 22 rows (adjust length here if desired).
Cast off loosely and evenly.
Row Sequence Rows 1 to 61(81) St st.
Make Garter Stitch ridge Next 2 rows Knit, Next
3 rows Purl, Next 2 rows Knit.
Row 69(89) (RS) Now refer to graph and starting at
position marked for Women's or Men's sleeve, work
rows 1 - 11, then repeat rows 8 - 11 inclusive
throughout for remainder.

POCKET LININGS (make 2)

Using 4.00mm needles cast on 33 sts.
Using St St, work 60 rows. Cast off.

MAKING UP

Press all pieces gently on WS using a warm iron over
a damp cloth. Using Backstitch, join shoulder seams.
Centre sleeves into armholes and join. Join sleeve
seams using Edge to Edge stitch on ribs.

Collar Using 4.00mm needles, cast on 182 sts.

Row 1 * K2, p2, rep from * to last 2 sts, k2.

Row 2 * P2, k2, rep from * to last 2 sts, p2.

Cont in k2, p2 rib for 6 rows.

Cast off 3 sts at beg of next 14 rows, then 4 sts at beg
of next 22 rows, keeping rib patt correct [52sts].

Cast off evenly in rib as set.

Using Edge to Edge stitch, attach cast off edge of
collar piece to neck hole.

Button band With RS facing using 3.75mm needles,
pick up knit 129 sts evenly along Left Front from
bottom edge to beg of neck shaping. Work 8 rows in
k2, p2 rib. Cast off evenly in rib. Mark position on
button band for 6 buttons, the first to come 2cm up
from lower edge, the last to come 2cm from beg of
neck shaping and the remainder spaced evenly
between. Sew on buttons.

Button hole band Work as for button band, making
button holes to correspond with position of buttons.

Pockets Slip stitch RS of pocket linings to WS of
Fronts on 3 sides, placing cast-on edge of lining to
top of ribbing and 60 rows along side edge of Front,
leaving this side edge open.

Using backstitch, join side seams, stitching both
pocket lining and Front to Back for 25 rows above
ribbing, then pocket lining only to Back for next 35
rows, then Fronts to Back for remainder.

Pocket edgings With RS facing, using 3.25mm
needles, pick up 32 sts evenly along side edge
(pocket) openings on Fronts. Knit 2 rows. Cast off.
Slip st side edge of pocket edgings into position,
overlapping Back. Press seams.

Brunswick Version 1, far right.

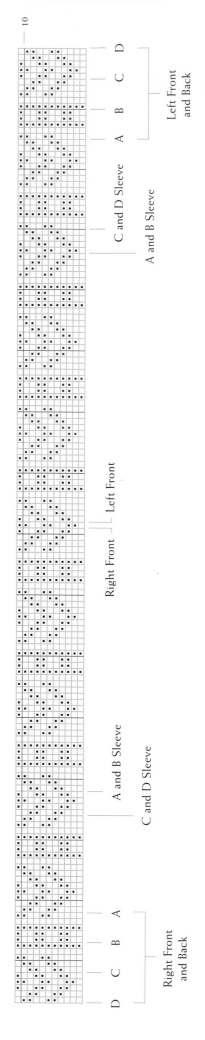

BRUNSWICK GRAPH
FRONT, BACK AND SLEEVES

DARJEELING

DARJEELING

Knitting Rating: Experienced Cable.

MEASUREMENTS

Women's Sizes	S	(M	L)
To fit bust	80	90	100 cm
Bodice circumference	104	114	124 cm
Bodice length	69	69	69 cm
Sleeve length	46	46	46 cm

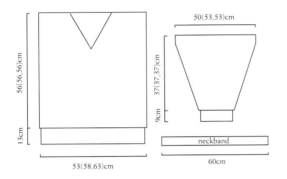

YARN

Jo Sharp 8ply DK Pure Wool Hand Knitting Yarn

Colour	Yarn Quantity		
Sizes	S	(M	L)
Version 1			
Gold 320	18	18	19 x 50g balls
Version 2			
Silk 903	18	18	19 x 50g balls

NEEDLES

1 pair 3.25mm (US 3) (UK 10)
1 pair 3.75mm (US 5) (UK 9)
1 pair 4.00mm (US 6) (UK 8)
1 Cable needle

TENSION

22.5 sts and 30 rows measured over 10cm Stocking Stitch, using 4.00mm needles.

SPECIAL ABBREVIATIONS

Work 5 tog (work 5 sts together) With yarn at back of work, slip 3sts purlwise, * pass 2nd st on right hand needle over 1st st (centre) st, slip centre st back to left hand needle, pass 2nd st on left hand needle over *, slip centre st back to right hand needle, rep from * to * once more, purl centre st. *(note; stitch referred to as 'centre st' is centre one of 5 sts)*

MB (make bobble) (K1, p1) twice all into next st, turn and p4, turn and sl 2, k2 tog, p2 sso (bobble completed).

M1K (make 1 st knitwise) Pick up strand of yarn lying between last st worked and next st, then knit into back of it.

M3 (make 3 sts) (K1, p1, k1) all into next st.

T3B (twist 3 back) Slip next st onto cable needle and hold at back of work, knit next 2 sts from left hand needle, then purl st from cable needle.

T3F (twist 3 front) Slip next 2 sts onto cable needle and hold at front of work, purl next st from left hand needle, then knit sts from cable needle.

T4B (twist 4 back) Slip next 2 sts onto cable needle and hold at back of work, knit next 2 sts from left hand needle, then purl sts from cable needle.

T4F (twist 4 front) Slip next 2 sts onto cable needle and hold at front of work, purl next 2 sts from left hand needle, then knit sts from cable needle.

C4B (cable 4 back) Slip next 2 sts onto cable needle and hold at back of work, knit next 2 sts from left hand needle, then knit sts from cable needle.

C4F (cable 4 front) Slip next 2 sts onto cable needle and hold at front of work, knit next 2 sts from left hand needle, then knit sts from cable needle.

Darjeeling Version 1, previous 2 pages
Darjeeling Version 2, left and top right

CABLE PANEL A

Worked over 12 sts
Row 1 (RS) *K6, p1, k4, p1, rep from *.
Row 2 *K1, p4, k1, p6, rep from *.
Row 3 *K6, p1, C4B, p1, rep from *.
Row 4 As row 2.
Repeat rows 3 & 4 to form pattern.

CABLE PANEL B

Worked over 38 sts
Row 1 (RS) P1, T3B, p4, T4B, p1, T4F, T4B, p12, T3B, p2.
Row 2 K3, p2, k14, p4, k5, p2, k5, p2, k1.
Row 3 T3B, p5, k2, p5, C4B, p13, T3B, p3.
Row 4 K4, p2, k13, p4, k5, p2, k6, p2.
Row 5 T3F, p2, MB, p2, T4F, p1, T4B, T4F, p11, T3F, p1, MB, p1.
Row 6 K3, p2, k12, p2, k4, p2, k1, p2, k7, p2, k1.
Row 7 P1, T3F, p6, work 5 tog, p4, T4F, p4, M1K, M3, M1K, p5, T3F, p2.
Row 8 K2, p2, k6, p2, k1, p2, k4, p2, k13, p2, k2.
Row 9 P2, T3F, p12, T4F, T4B, p1, T4F, P4, T3F, p1.
Row 10 K1, p2, k5, p2, k5, p4, k14, p2, k3.
Row 11 P3, T3F, p13, C4F, p5, k2, p5, T3F.
Row 12 P2, k6, p2, k5, p4, k13, p2, k4.
Row 13 P1, MB, p1, T3B, p11, T4B, T4F, p1, T4B, p2, MB, p2 T3B.
Row 14 K1, p2, k7, p2, k1, p2, k4, p2, k12, p2, k3.
Row 15 P2, T3B, p5, M1K, M3, M1K, p4, T4B, p4, work 5 tog, p6, T3B, p1.
Row 16 K2, p2, k13, p2, k4, p2, k1, p2, k6, p2, k2.

FRONT

Using 3.25mm needle cast on 132(144,156)sts. Work 4 rows K1, p1 rib.
Change to 3.75mm needles, using Cable Panel A, work 11cm (ending on a WS row).
Change to 4.00mm needles.
Row 1 (RS) P8(14,21)sts, work row 1 of Cable Panel B, p40sts, rep row 1 Cable Panel B, p8(14,21)sts [132(144,156)sts].
Row 2 K 8(14,21)sts, work row 2 Cable Panel B, k40 sts, rep row 2 Cable Panel B, K8(14,21)sts.
These 2 rows form patt placement throughout.
Keeping patt correct work * 104 rows.
Shape Neck, next row (RS)Work 66(72,78)sts, turn leave rem 66(72,78)sts on holder. Work each side of neck separately. Dec 1 st at neck edge on next row, then foll 3rd row 15 times, then foll 4th row twice. Work 9 rows straight. Cast off loosely and evenly [48(54,60)sts].
Rejoin yarn to rem sts and complete second side to match first side, rev all shaping.

BACK

Work as for front to * then cont until back bodice length matches front bodice. Cast off.

Darjeeling Version 1

SLEEVES

Using 3.25mm needles, cast on 66(72,72)sts.
Work 4 rows k1, p1 rib.
Change to 3.75mm needle and using Cable Panel A, 7 cm (ending on a WS row).
Change to 4.00mm needles and work in reverse st st throughout AT THE SAME TIME **Shape Sleeves** inc 1 st at each end of next row, then foll 4th row 20(18,18)times, then foll alt rows 0(5,5)times [108(120,120)sts]. Work 31(29,29)rows straight (112 rows) *(adjust length here if desired)*. Cast off loosely and evenly.

MAKING UP

Press all pieces gently on WS using a warm iron over a damp cloth. Using Backstitch, join shoulder seams, centre sleeves and join. Join side and sleeve seam using Edge to Edge stitch on ribs.
Neckband Using 3.25mm needles, cast on 174 sts and work 4 rows k1, p1 rib. Change to 3.75mm needles and working in Cable Panel A, work 4cm. Cast off.
Pin neckband into V neck opening, stretching slightly to fit. Sew into place using Edge to Edge stitch and overlapping front edges to create cross over effect at front. Press seams.

Darjeeling Version 2, right

EBONY

EBONY

Knitting Rating: Beginner Knitter

MEASUREMENTS

Unisex Sizing	A	(B	C	D)	
To fit chest / bust	85	95	105	115	cm
Bodice Circumference	116	126	136	144	cm
Bodice Length	69	69	69	69	cm
Sleeve length	42	42	48	48	cm

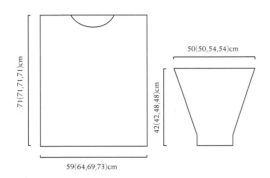

71(71,71,71)cm

50(50,54,54)cm

42(42,48,48)cm

59(64,69,73)cm

YARN

Jo Sharp 8ply DK Pure Wool Hand Knitting Yarn

No.	Colour	Yarn Quantity				
Size		A	(B	C	D)	
Version 1						
Col 1	Winter 904	17	17	18	19	x 50g balls
Col 2	Ebony 902	5	6	6	6	x 50g balls
Version 2						
Col 1	Ebony 902	17	17	18	19	x 50g balls
Col 2	Owl 801	5	6	6	6	x 50g balls

NEEDLES

1 pair 3.75mm needles (USA 5) (UK 9)
1 pair 4.00mm (USA 6) (UK 8)
Version 1 - 4.50mm circular needles (USA 7) (UK 7)
Version 2 - 3.75mm circular needles (USA 5) (UK 9)

TENSION

21 stitches and 38 rows measured over 10cm of Moss
Stitch pattern using 4.00mm needles.

MOSS STITCH PATTERN

Row 1 K1 p1 to end.
Row 2 P all the k sts and k all the p sts as they face
you. Rep row 2.

COLOUR SEQUENCE

Work 20 rows in col 1 then *work 2 rows col 1,
and 2 rows col 2, rep from * 9 times.
Repeat these 60 rows.

Ebony Version 1, left
Ebony Version 1 & 2 previous page, left
Ebony Version 2, previous page, right

BACK

Using 3.75 mm needle and col 1, cast on
125(135,145,155)sts, working in Moss St & **Colour
Sequence** throughout, work 20 rows. Change to
4.00mm needles and work a further 218 rows. Now
working in col 1 for the remainder of the Back, * work
24(24,20,20)rows *(adjust length here if desired, ending on WS
row)*.
Shape Back Neck (RS) Work 62(67,72,77)sts, leave
rem 63(68,73,78)sts on holder, turn, cast off 7 sts at
beg of next row, then foll alt row twice. Work
2(2,6,6)rows straight [270 rows]. Cast off rem
41(46,49,54)sts.
With (RS) facing rejoin yarn to rem sts.
Cast off 8 sts at beg of first row, then 7 sts at neck
edge on foll alt rows, twice. Work 2(2,6,6)rows
straight [270 rows]. Cast off rem 41(46,49,54)sts.

FRONT

Work as for back to * work 10(10,6,6)rows.
Shape Front Neck (RS) Work 62(67,72,77)sts, leave
rem 63(68,73,78)sts on holder, Work each side of
neck separately.
Cast of 10(10,9,9) sts at beg of next row, then 2sts at
neck edge of every alt row 4(4,5,5)times, then dec 1
st on every alt row 1(1,3,3)times [41(46,48,53)sts]
[262(262,264,264)rows]. Work 8(8,6,6)rows straight
[270 rows]. Cast off loosely and evenly.
With RS facing, rejoin yarn to rem sts and cast off
11(11,10,10)sts at beg of next row, then 2sts at neck
edge of every alt row 4(4,5,5)times, then dec 1 st on
every alt row 1(1,3,3)times [41(46,48,53)sts]
[262(262,264,264)rows]. Work 8(8,6,6)rows straight
[270 rows]. Cast off loosely and evenly.

SLEEVE

*It is advised, when knitting this unisex garment for a man, to use
the size "D" sleeve.*
Sleeve is to be worked throughout in Moss Stitch.
Follow **Colour Sequence** for the first 120 rows of
sleeve, then complete in Col 1.
Using 3.75 mm needle and Col 1, cast on
59(59,69,69)sts. Patt 10 rows. Change to 4.00mm
needles.
Shape sleeve Inc 1 st at each end of foll 5(5,6,6)th
rows, 20 times, then every 9(9,13,13)th row 3 times
[105(105,115,115)sts] [137(137,169,169) rows].
Work 22(22,20,20) rows straight *(adjust length here is
desired)*. Cast off loosely and evenly.

MAKING UP

Using Backstitch, join shoulder seams, centre
sleeves and join. Join side and sleeve seam.

Make collar *(Version 1 & 2 given)*

Long Cowl Collar (shown on Version 1)
With RS facing, using 4.50mm circular needle and
col 1, pick up and knit 126(126,133, 133)sts evenly
around neckhole and work in Moss Stitch until
collar measures 16cm in length. Cast off.

Short Crew Collar (shown on Version 2)
With RS facing, using 3.75mm circular needle and
col 1, pick up and knit 126(126,133, 133)sts evenly
around neckhole and work in Moss Stitch until
collar measures 7cm in length. Cast off.

Ebony Version 1, above
Ebony Version 2, right

EMPORIUM

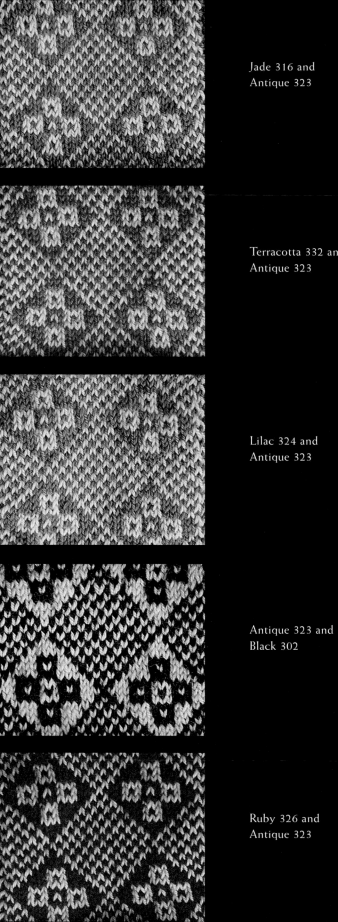

Jade 316 and
Antique 323

Terracotta 332 an
Antique 323

Lilac 324 and
Antique 323

Antique 323 and
Black 302

Ruby 326 and
Antique 323

EMPORIUM

Knitting Rating: Experienced in Fairisle.

MEASUREMENTS

Women's Sizes	S	(M	L	XL)	
To fit chest	80	90	100	110	cm
Bodice circumference	98	108	118	128	cm
Bodice length	58	58	58	58	cm
Sleeve length (folded)	49	49	49	49	cm

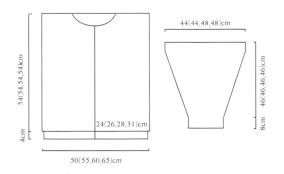

YARN

Jo Sharp 8 ply DK Pure Wool Hand Knitting Yarn

No.	Key	Colour		Yarn Quantity		
Sizes			S	(M	L	XL)
Version 1						
Col 1		Linen 335	13	13	13	14	x 50g balls
Col 2	·	Navy 327	2	2	3	3	x 50g balls
Version 2						
Col 1		Ebony 902	13	13	13	14	x 50g balls
Col 2	·	Silk 903	2	2	3	3	x 50g balls

Additional colourways, shown left.
All examples shown at left use Jo Sharp 8ply DK Pure Wool Hand Knitting Yarn. The shades used are identified at right of each illustration.

Emporium Version 1, previous page, left and right.

Emporium additional colourways, left.

Emporium Version 2, top right.

NEEDLES
1 pair 3.25mm (USA 3) (UK 10)
1 x 4.00 mm (USA 6) (UK 8)

BUTTONS
Version 1 - 7 x 1.5 cm diameter
Version 2 - 7 x 2 cm diameter (DV 3 Durango)
See page 107 for 'Durango Buttons' address.

TENSION
Measured over 10cm with 4.00mm needles.
Fairisle 25 sts & 25 rows.
Moss Stitch 20.5 sts & 38 rows.

MOSS STITCH PATTERN
Work in K1 P1 across first row, then on all subsequent rows, k all the p sts and p all the k sts, as they face you.

LEFT FRONT
Using 3.25mm needles and Col 1 cast on 53(59,63,71)sts. Work 15 rows Moss st.
Row 16 (WS) Inc 6 sts evenly across row 59(65,69,77)sts.
Change to 4.00mm needles.
Now refer to graph for pattern and placement and cont until work measures 46(46,44,44)cm inclusive of band and ending with a WS row.
Shape Neck Cast off 4(4,4,4)sts at neck edge of next row then 2(2,2,2)sts on next and foll alt rows 2(2,3,3)times, then 1(1,1,1)st on every row 8(8,8,8)times [43(49,51,59)sts]. Work 6(6,8,8)rows
Cast off loosely.

RIGHT FRONT

Work as for Left Front reversing all shaping.

BACK

Using 3.25 mm needles and Col 1 , cast on
103(113,123,133)sts. Work 16 rows of Moss Stitch.
Change to 4.00mm needles and cont in Moss St. until
back bodice length matches front bodice. Cast off.

SLEEVES

Using 4.00 mm needles and Col 1 throughout cast on
49(49,53,53)sts. Work 30 rows Moss st.
Shape Sleeves Keeping Moss stitch patt correct, inc
1 st at each end of every 7th row 18(18,20,20)times,
then every 8(8,4,4)th row, 3 times [91(91,99,99)sts].
Work 23(23,19,19)rows straight *(adjust length here if
desired)*. Cast off loosely.

MAKING UP

Press all pieces, very gently on WS using a warm iron
over a damp cloth, taking care not to flatten Moss
Stitch texture. Using Backstitch, join shoulder seams.
Centre sleeves and join. Using Backstitch join sleeve
seams, reversing seam for first 18 rows of each cuff.
Fold cuffs back.

Button Band Using 3.25mm needles and Col 1, cast
on 7 sts. Work in Moss st until band (when slightly
stretched) is the same length as the front, to beg of
neck shaping. Sew band into position as you go.
Leave 7 sts on the stitch holder at neckline. Mark
position on band for 7 buttons, the first to come 2cm
from lower edge, the last to come 2cm from top of
band, the other 5 spaced evenly between.
Buttonhole Band Cast on 7sts and work to
correspond with Button Band, keeping Moss st Pattern
correct, and working 7 button holes opposite markers
as follows; work 2sts, cast off 3sts, work 2sts. On
next row, cast on 3 sts in place of those cast off on
previous row.
Collar With RS facing, using 3.25mm needles and
col 1, pick up 7 sts from right front stitch
holder,22(22,26,26)sts up right front neck,
25(25,29,29)sts across back neck, 22(22,26,26)sts
down left front neck and 7 sts from holder at left
front neck [83(83,95,95)sts]. Using Col 1, work 34
rows in Moss st. Cast off.

EMPORIUM GRAPH

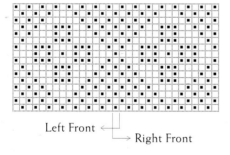

Left Front ←
→ Right Front

*Note: Pattern repeat is to be worked from centre
marking towards the left or right.*

Emporium Version 2, right.

52

GEORGIA

Knitting Rating; Average.

MEASUREMENTS

Women's Sizes	S	(M	L	XL)	
To fit bust	80	90	100	110	cm
Bodice circumference	92	103	114	126	cm
Bodice length	65	66	67	68	cm
Sleeve length	40	40	40	40	cm

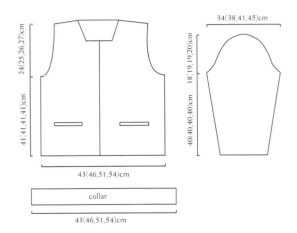

YARN

Jo Sharp 8ply DK Pure Wool Hand Knitting Yarn

Colour		Yarn Quantity			
Sizes	S	(M	L	XL)	
Version 1					
Forest 318	20	20	21	21	x 50 g balls
Version 2					
Heron 802	20	20	21	21	x 50 g balls

NEEDLES

1 pair 3.25mm (UK 10) (USA 3)
1 pair 4.00mm (UK 8) (USA 6)
A cable needle

BUTTONS

3 x 2.5 cm diameter.

TENSION

28 sts and 32 rows to 10cm, measured over patt using 4.00mm Needles.

SPECIAL ABBREVIATIONS

TwR - knit into front of 2nd st on left-hand needle,then into front of first, slipping both sts off needle tog.
Cr3 - slip next 2 sts onto cable needle and leave at back of work, knit next st on left-hand needle, slip one st from left-hand end of cable needle onto left-hand needle and knit this st, then knit rem st from cable needle.

Georgia Version 1, previous 2 pages
Georgia Version 2, left & right

BACK

Using 3.25mm Needles, cast on 104(118,130,142)sts. Knit 5 rows garter st (1st row is WS).
Row 6 K2(5,3,1), inc knitways in next st, * k3, inc knitways in next st, rep from *to last 1(4,2,0)st/s, k1(4,2,0) [130(146,162,178)sts]. Change to 4.00mm Needles.
Begin Pattern Row 1 (WS) Purl.
Row 2 K2, * (TwR) 3 times, k2, rep from * to end.
Row 3 Purl.
Row 4 K2, * (Cr3) twice, k2, rep from * to end.
These 4 rows form patt throughout. Work a further 121 rows patt, thus ending with a first row [125 rows patt in all].
Shape armholes Keeping patt correct, cast off 6(8,10,12)sts at beg of next 2 rows [118(130,142,154)sts].
Dec 1 st at each end of next and alt rows 6(7,10,11) times in all [106(116,122,132)sts]. Work 63(65,63,63) rows patt.
Shape shoulders Cast off 12(13,13,14)sts at beg of next 4 rows, then 11(12,14,15)sts at beg of foll 2 rows.
Cast off rem 36(40,42,46)sts.

POCKET LININGS (make 2)

Using 4.00mm Needles, cast on 34 sts.
Work 50 rows stocking st, inc 8 sts evenly across last row [42 sts]. Leave sts on a stitch holder.

KALEIDOSCOPE

Knitting Rating: Beginner

MEASUREMENTS
Cropped & Classic Vests

Unisex Sizing	A	(B	C	D)	
To fit chest / bust	90	100	110	120	cm
Finished Bodice width	110	120	132	144	cm
Bodice classic length	69	69	69	69	cm
Bodice cropped length	51	51	51	51	cm

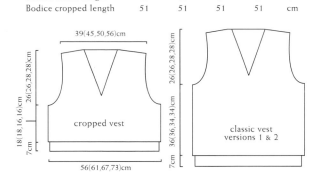

Adult Sweaters

Unisex Sizing	A	(B	C	D)	
To fit chest / bust	90	100	110	120	cm
Finished Bodice width	110	120	132	144	cm
Bodice Length	68	68	68	68	cm
Sleeve (set in)	42	42	46	46	cm

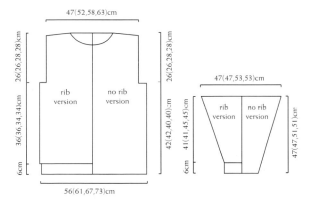

Children's Sweaters

Unisex Sizing	1-2	(3-5	6-8	7-9	10-12)	
To fit chest	55	60	65	70	75	cm
Finished Bodice width	76	78	90	100	110	cm
Bodice Length	35	40	46	51	56	cm
Sleeve	24	27	29	32	36	cm

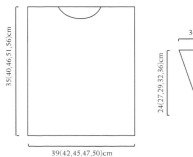 

Kaleidoscope Cropped Vest, left

YARN
Jo Sharp 8 ply DK Pure Wool Hand Knitting Yarn.
Adult Garments

No.	Colour	Yarn quantity				
Sizes		A	(B	C	D)	

Cropped Vest

No.	Colour	A	(B	C	D)	
Col 1	Orchard 906	2	2	2	2	x 50g balls
Col 2	Antique 323	2	2	2	2	x 50g balls
Col 3	Winter 904	6	6	7	7	x 50g balls
Col 4	Renaissance 312	2	2	2	2	x 50g balls
Col 5	Citrus 509	2	2	2	2	x 50g balls

Classic Vest Version 1

Col 1	Owl 801	2	2	2	3	x 50g balls
Col 2	Slate 328	2	3	3	3	x 50g balls
Col 3	Wine 307	6	6	7	7	x 50g balls
Col 4	Cherry 309	2	2	2	3	x 50g balls
Col 5	Forest 318	2	2	3	3	x 50g balls

Classic Vest Version 2

Col 1	Slate 328	2	2	2	3	x 50g balls
Col 2	Embers 804	2	3	3	3	x 50g balls
Col 3	Navy 327	6	6	7	7	x 50g balls
Col 4	Aegean 504	2	2	2	3	x 50g balls
Col 5	Wine 307	2	2	3	3	x 50g balls

Adult Sweater Version 1 *(without rib)*

Col 1	Monsoon 704	2	3	3	3	x 50g balls
Col 2	Khaki 329	2	3	3	3	x 50g balls
Col 3	Ebony 902	10	10	10	11	x 50g balls
Col 4	Navy 327	2	2	2	3	x 50g balls
Col 5	Linen 335	2	3	3	3	x 50g balls

Adult Sweater Version 2 *(with rib)*

Col 1	Owl 801	2	2	3	3	x 50g balls
Col 2	Black 302	2	3	3	3	x 50g balls
Col 3	Smoke 339	11	12	12	12	x 50g balls
Col 4	Embers 804	2	2	2	3	x 50g balls
Col 5	Mulberry 325	2	3	3	3	x 50g balls

Children's Garments

Unisex Sizing	1-2	(3-5	6-8	7-9	10-12)	

Children's Sweater Version 1

		1-2	(3-5	6-8	7-9	10-12)	
Col 1	Plum 505	1	1	2	2	2	x 50g balls
Col 2	Coral 304	1	2	2	2	2	x 50g balls
Col 3	Embers 804	5	5	5	5	6	x 50g balls
Col 4	Chartreuse 330	1	1	2	2	2	x 50g balls
Col 5	Renaissance 312	1	2	2	2	2	x 50g balls

Children's Sweater Version 2

		1-2	(3-5	6-8	7-9	10-12)	
Col 1	Jade 316	1	1	2	2	2	x 50g balls
Col 2	Miro 507	1	2	2	2	2	x 50g balls
Col 3	Ebony 902	5	5	5	5	6	x 50g balls
Col 4	Cherry 309	1	1	2	2	2	x 50g balls
Col 5	Embers 804	1	2	2	2	2	x 50g balls

Kaleidoscope Sweater Version 1, left & right

KALEIDOSCOPE CHILDREN'S SWEATERS

FRONT

Using 3.75mm needles and col 1, cast on 84(90,96,102,108)sts. Working in Texture Pattern (page 71) * work 29(34,39,44,49)cm ending with a WS row.

Shape Neck Work 37(40,42,45,48)sts, turn and leave rem 47(50,54,57,60)sts on a holder. Work each side of neck separately. Dec 1 st at neck edge of every alt row 8(8,9,9,9)times. Work 9(9,10,10,10)rows straight. Cast off rem 29(32,33,36,39)sts.

With RS facing, leave 10(10,12,12,12)sts on holder, rejoin yarn to rem sts and complete second side to match first side, rev all shaping.

BACK

Work as for front to * cont until Back Bodice length matches Front Bodice length. Cast off loosely and evenly.

SLEEVES

Using 3.25mm needles and Col 3, cast on 42(42,48,48,48)sts. Knit 3 rows.

Change to 3.75mm needles and begin Texture Pattern, replacing all colour changes with col 3 AT THE SAME TIME **Shape Sleeve** Keeping patt correct, inc 1 st at each end of every 4(5,6,6,7)th row, 18 times [78(78,84,84,84)sts] [75(93,111,111,129)total rows].

Work 33(28,19,32,32)rows straight. Cast off loosely and evenly.

MAKING UP

Using Backstitch, join shoulder seams. Centre sleeves and join. Join side and sleeve seams.

Neckband With RS facing, using 3.75mm needles and col 3, pick up and k 20(20,24,24,24) sts down left front neck, 10(10,12,12,12)sts from st holder at centre front, 20(20,24,24,24)sts up right front neck and 26(26,30,30,30)sts at back neck 76(76,90,90,90)sts.

Row 1 & 2 Purl, **Row 3 & 4** Knit, **Row 5** Purl. **Next row** (WS) Purl.

Cont in St st for 3 rows, thread sts onto piece of yarn. Fold collar to inside and sew down evenly, catching and sewing sts from holder along the way. When complete, remove contrast yarn holder. Press seams.

Note; leaving sts on a holder and sewing down without casting off makes neckhole more flexible.

Kaleidoscope Children's Sweaters
Versions 1 & 2, right

Paragon Version 1

PARAGON

Knitting Rating; Beginner Knitter with knowledge of Intarsia.

MEASUREMENTS

Women's Sizes	S	(M	L	XL)	
To fit bust	80	90	100	110	cm
Bodice circumference	100	110	120	132	cm
Bodice length	69	69	69	69	cm
Sleeve length	43	43	43	43	cm

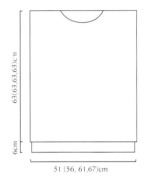

YARN

Jo Sharp 8 ply DK Pure Wool Hand Knitting Yarn

No.	Key	Colour					Yarn Quantity			
Sizes							S	(M	L	XL)

Women's Version 1

Col 1	☐	Orchard 906	12	13	13	13	x 50g balls
	■	Winter 904	3	3	4	4	x 50g balls
	⊠	Amethyst 503	1	1	2	2	x 50g balls
	◣	Avocado 337	1	1	1	1	x 50g ball

Women's Version 2

Col 1	☐	Winter 904	14	15	15	15	x 50g balls
Col 2	◣	Orchard 906	1	1	2	2	x 50g balls

NEEDLES

1 pair 3.75mm (USA 5) (UK 9)
1 pair 4.00mm (USA 6) (UK 8)
3.75mm circular needle (USA 5) (UK 9)
Stitch Holder

TENSION

22.5 sts and 30 rows to 10cm measured over Stocking Stitch and Intarsia using 4.00mm needles.

BACK

Using 3.75mm needles and col 1, cast on 114(126,138,150)sts. Work in k2, p2 rib for 18 rows. Change to 4.00mm needles and using st st, beg with a K row, foll graph for col changes for version 1 *(for Version 2, work all graph symbols in col 1, except inverted triangle symbol used on the cross motif, which is to be worked in col 2).* Work 190 rows. Cast off.

Paragon Version 2

FRONT

Work as given for Back to *. Work 168 rows
Shape Neck Work 45(51,57,63)sts, turn and leave rem sts on a holder. Work each side of neck separately. Cast off 2 sts at neck edge on next row and foll alt rows twice and 1 st on foll alt rows 3 times [36(42,48,54)sts] [180 rows]. Work 10 rows, cast off. With RS facing, leave 24 sts on holder, rejoin yarn to rem sts and complete second side to match first side, rev all shaping.

SLEEVES

One sleeve, all sizes.
Using 3.75mm needles and col 1, cast on 54 sts
Work in k2, p2 rib for 18 rows, inc 11 sts evenly across last row [65 sts]. Change to 4.00mm needles and using st st, beg with a k row, foll graph for col changes for version 1 *(for Version 2, work all graph symbols in col 1, except inverted triangle symbol used on the cross motif, which is to be worked in col 2)* AT THE SAME TIME shape sides by inc 1 st at each end of 7th row and every foll 5th row, 19 times [105 sts]. Work 8 rows [110 rows] *(adjust length here if desired).* Cast off loosely and evenly.

MAKING UP

Press all pieces, except ribbing, gently on WS using a warm iron over a damp cloth. Using Backstitch, join shoulder seams. Centre sleeves and join. Join side and sleeve seams using Edge to Edge stitch on ribs**.
Neckband With RS facing, using a 3.75mm circular needle and col 1, pick up and k 28 sts down left side front neck, 24 sts from st holder at centre front, 28 sts up right side front neck and 44 sts across back neck (124 sts). Work k2, p2 rib for 11 rounds. Knit 8 rounds, cast off. Press seams.

PRECIOUS JEWEL

PRECIOUS JEWEL

Knitting Rating - Experienced in Intarsia.

MEASUREMENTS

Women's Sizes	S	(M	L	XL)	
To fit chest/bust	80	90	100	110	cm
Bodice circumference	104	116	122	134	cm
Bodice length (cardigan)	76	76	76	76	cm
Bodice length (sweater)	48	48	48	48	cm
Sleeve length	45	45	50	50	cm

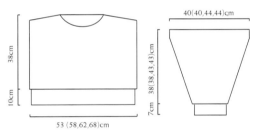

YARN

Jo Sharp 8 ply DK Pure Wool Hand Knitting Yarn

No.	Key	Colour	S	(M	L	XL)	
Sizes							Yarn Quantity
Cardigan							
Col 1	☐	Ink 901	6	7	7	7	x 50g balls
Col 2	■	Navy 327	6	6	6	6	x 50g balls
Col 3	+	Violet 319	5	5	5	5	x 50g balls
	◢	Lichen 803	3	3	3	3	x 50g balls
	✕	Aegean 504	1	1	1	1	x 50g ball
	♥	Coral 304	1	1	1	1	x 50g ball
	◥	Lilac 324	1	1	1	1	x 50g ball
	⬚	Chartreuse 330	1	1	1	1	x 50g ball
Sweater							
Col 1	☐	Ebony 902	5	5	5	5	x 50g balls
Col 2	■	Embers 804	6	6	6	6	x 50g balls
Col 3	+	Storm 706	4	4	5	5	x 50g balls
Col 4	◢	Miro 507	2	2	2	2	x 50g balls
	✕	Ginger 322	1	1	1	1	x 50g ball
	♥	Gold 320	1	1	1	1	x 50g ball
	◥	Chestnut 506	1	1	1	1	x 50g ball
	⬚	Aegean 504	1	1	1	1	x 50g ball

Precious Jewel Cardigan, left.
Precious Jewel Sweater, previous 2 pages.

NEEDLES

1 pair 3.25mm (USA 3) (UK 10)
1 pair 3.75mm (USA 5) (UK 9)
1 pair 4.00mm (USA 6) (UK 8)

BUTTONS

Cardigan - 7 x 2cm diameter

TENSION

22.5 sts and 30 rows measured over 10cm of Stocking Stitch & Intarsia using 4.00 mm needles.

CARDIGAN

LEFT FRONT

Using 3.75mm needles and col 1, cast on 60(66,70,76)sts. Work 7cm in k2, p2 rib. Change to 4.00mm needles and refer to graph for colour changes, cont until work measures 68cm inclusive of rib and ending with a RS row.
Shape Neck (WS) Keeping patt correct, cast off 5 sts and work to end of row. Cast off 2 sts at neck edge of next row, then every alt row, 4 times, then 1 st every alt row, 3 times [42(48,52,58)sts].
Shape Shoulder (RS) Cast off 14(16,17,19)sts at beg of next and foll alt row, work 1 row, cast off rem 14(16,18,20)sts.

RIGHT FRONT

Work Right Front to match Left Front, rev all shaping.

BACK

Using 3.75mm needles and col 1, cast on 120(132,140,152)sts. Make rib as for Front and follow graph until back bodice length matches front bodice length, incorporating shoulder shaping on last 6 rows as follows;
Shape Shoulders Cast off 14(16,17,19)sts at beg of next 4 rows then 14(16,18,20)sts at beg of next 2 rows. Leave rem 36sts on a holder.

SLEEVES

Using 3.25mm needles and col 3, cast on 47(47,57,57)sts. Work in k2 p2 rib for 7cm increasing 11 sts in last WS row [58(58,68,68)sts].
Change to 4.00mm needles and refer to graph for colour changes, substituting col 1 for col 2 and visa versa throughout.
AT THE SAME TIME **Shape Sleeve** Inc 1 st at each end of every 5(5,6,6)th row 12 times, then every 8(8,9,9)th row 4 times [90(90,100,100)sts] [92(92,108,108)rows]. Work 22(22,21,21)rows straight *(adjust length here if desired)*. Cast off.

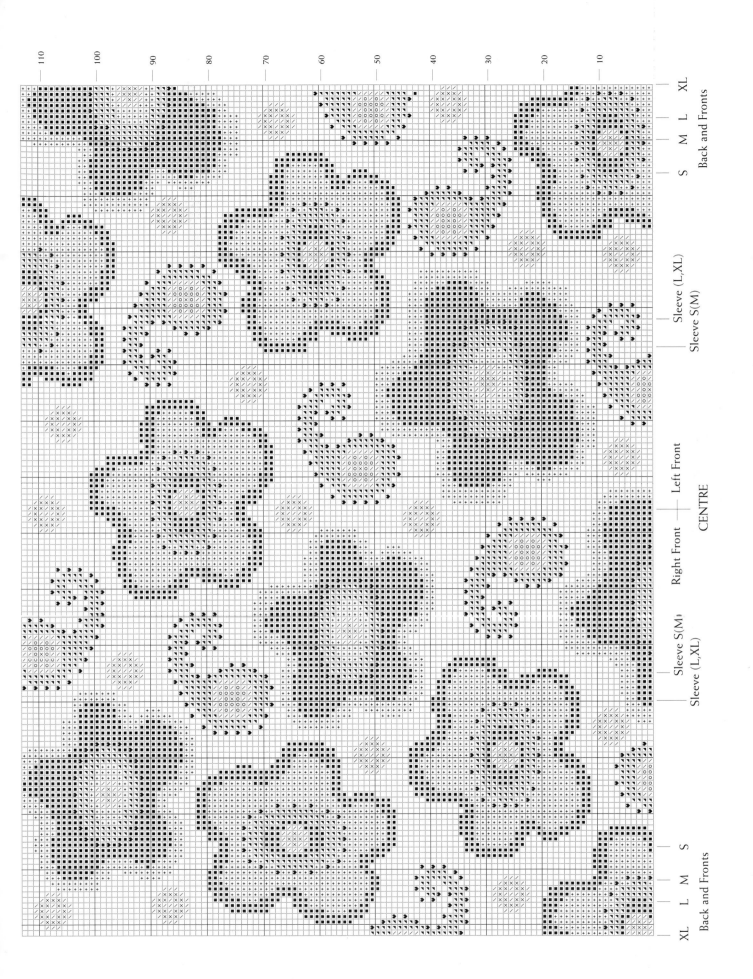

93

MAKING UP

Press all pieces gently on WS using a warm iron over a damp cloth. Using Backstitch, join shoulder seams. Centre sleeves and join. Join side and sleeve seams using Edge to Edge stitch on ribs.

Button Band Using 3.25mm needles and Col 3, pick up 158 sts evenly along left front edge. Work 3 rows k2 p2 rib. Change to col 2 and cont in rib for a further 6 rows. Cast off in rib. Mark position on band for 7 buttons, the first to come 2cm from lower edge, the last to come 2cm from top of band, the other 5 spaced evenly between. Sew on buttons.

Buttonhole Band Make right front band to correspond with left band with 7 button holes opposite markers.

Collar With RS facing, using 3.25mm needles and col 2, pick up 6 sts along top of right front band, 28 sts up right front neck, 36 sts from back neck stitch holder, 28 sts down left front neck, and 6 sts along top of left front band [104 sts]. Work in k1, p1 rib, until collar measures 10cm. Cast off. Press seams.

SWEATER

FRONT

Using 3.75mm needles and col 2, cast on 120(132,140,152)sts. Work 2 rows k2, p2 rib. Change to col 3, work a further 2 rows rib. Change to col 2 and cont in rib until band measures 10cm. Change to 4.00mm needles and cont on graph until bodice length, including band measures 42cm, ending on a WS row.

Shape Neck (RS) Work 53(59,63,69)sts, turn and leave rem 67(73,77,83)sts on a stitch holder. Cast off 3 sts at beg of next row, then every alt row 3(3,4,4)times, then 2 sts on next alt row 1(1,2,2)times, then 1(1,0,0,)sts on foll alt row [38(44,44,50)sts]. Work 0(0,1,1)row.

Shape Shoulder Cast off 13(14,14,16)sts on next and foll alt row.

Work 1 row.

Cast off rem 14(16,16,18)sts.

With RS facing, slip centre 14 sts onto a stitch holder, rejoin yarn to rem sts and complete second side to match first side rev all shaping.

BACK

Work Back bodice length to match Front bodice length, incorporating shoulder shaping on last 6 rows as follows;

Shape Shoulders Cast off 12(14,14,16)sts at beg of next 4 rows then 14(16,16,18)sts at beg of next 2 rows. Leave rem 44(44,52,52)sts on a holder.

SLEEVES

Work as for Cardigan sleeves, using col 1 on rib and reversing colours as per sweater.

MAKING UP

Press all pieces gently on WS using a warm iron over a damp cloth. Using backstitch, join shoulder seams. Centre sleeves and join. Join side and sleeve seams.

Neckband With RS facing, 3.25mm needles and col 3, pick up and k 23(23,25,25)sts down left front neck, 14 sts from stitch holder at front, 23(23,25,25)sts up right front and 44(44,52,52)sts across back neck. Work 12 rounds of k1, p1 rib. Change to col 2 and work a further 2 rows rib. Cast off in rib. Press seams.

Pillow Version 1, bottom left
Pillow Version 2, top right
Pillow Version 3, top centre
Pillow Version 4, bottom centre
Throw, bottom right

SERENDIPITY

Knitting rating;
Pillow Version 1 & 2 - Intarsia Knowledge
Pillow Version 3 & 4 - Beginner Knitter
Throw - Average Skilled

MEASUREMENTS

Throw
Width 125cm x Length 150cm (excluding fringe).

Pillows (all versions)
Width 46 cm x Length 52cm.

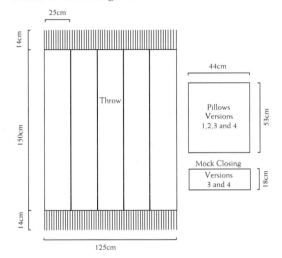

YARN
Jo Sharp 8 ply DK Pure Wool Hand Knitting Yarn.

No.	Colour	Yarn Quantity
Pillow	**Version 1**	
Col 1	Owl 801	6 x 50g balls
Col 2	Avocado 337	1 x 50g ball
Col 3	Terracotta 332	1 x 50g ball
Col4	Heron 802	1 x 50g ball
Col 5	Brick 333	1 x 50g ball
Pillow	**Version 2**	
Col 1	Heron 802	6 x 50g balls
Col 2	Avocado 337	1 x 50g ball
Col 3	Terracotta 332	1 x 50g ball
Col4	Owl 801	1 x 50g ball
Col 5	Brick 333	1 x 50g ball
Pillow	**Version 3**	
	Owl 801	7 x 50g balls
Pillow	**Version 4**	
	Heron 802	7 x 50g balls
Throw		
Col 1	Owl 801	24 x 50g balls
Col 2	Heron 802	15 x 50g balls

NEEDLES
1 pair 4.00mm (USA 6) (UK 8)

PILLOW STUFFING
Pillows all - 56 x 56 cm Cushion Insert

BUTTONS
6 x 2.5cm buttons

TENSION
Pillows - 22.5 sts and 30 rows to 10cm measured over Stocking stitch using 4.00mm needles.
Throw - 30 sts and 30 rows to 10cm measured over Stitch Pattern using 4.00mm needles.

PILLOWS - VERSIONS 1 & 2

TEXTURE & COLOUR PATTERN
24 row stitch and colour pattern.
Row 1 P4 Col 1, k8 Col 2, * p8 Col 1, k4 Col 3, p8 Col 1, k8 Col 2, rep from * to last p4 Col 1.
Row 2 K4 Col 1, p8 col 2, *k8 Col 1, p4 Col 3, k8 Col 1, p8 Col 2, rep from * to last k4 Col 1.
Rep row 1 and 2 twice
Row 7 Col 1, p4, k8, *p8 k4, p8, k8, rep from * to last p4.
Work 5 rows rev St st.
Row 13 P6 Col 1, k4 Col 5, *p8 Col 1, k8 Col 4, p8 Col 1, k4 Col 5, rep from * to last p6 Col 1.
Row 14 K6 Col 1, p4 Col 5, *k8 Col 1, p8 Col 4, k8 Col 1, p4 col 5, rep from * to last k6 Col 1.
Rep rows 13 & 14 twice
Row 19 P6 Col 1, k4, *p8, k8, p8, k4, rep from * to last p6.
Work 5 rows rev St st in Col 1 (24 rows).

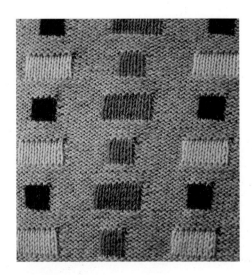

Pillow, Version 2

97

FRONT COVER PIECE

Using 4.00mm needles and Col 1, cast on 100 sts and work 4 rows rev St St.
Now refer to Texture & Colour Pattern and rep 6 times in all, then work rows 1 to 7 once. Work 3 rows in rev St st with Col 1 [158 rows]. Cast off.

BACK COVER PIECE

Using 4.00mm needles and Col 1, cast on 100 sts. Work 156 rows (or until back length matches front) in rev St St. Cast off.

MAKING UP

Using Edge to Edge stitch, with WS facing, join three sides of the Front and Back together. Reverse Stocking Stitch faces the front on back piece. Fill with cushion insert and join remaining side.

PILLOWS - VERSIONS 3 & 4

BACK & FRONT PIECE

Using 4.00mm needles, cast on 100 sts and work 158 rows St st, for first side of pillow. Cast off.
Make second side of pillow to match the first side.

MOCK CLOSING

Using 4.00mm needles, cast on 100 sts and work 8 rows in Garter Stitch (knit all rows).
Begin Patt
Row 1 Knit.
Row 2 K 6, p 88, k 6.
Rep rows 1 & 2, 20 times.
Work 8 rows Garter Stitch, cast off evenly.

Throw, This page below.
Pillows Versions 3 & 4 & Throw detail, opposite.

MAKING UP

Make up as per instructions for Pillows, Versions 1 & 2 with Reverse Stocking Stitch facing outside of pillow.
Press Mock Closing piece firmly and attach to pillow at top and sew buttons in place (as shown in illustration).

THROW

STITCH PATTERN

Row 1 (RS) P2, *kb1, k1, p1, kb1, p2, rep from * to end.
Row 2 K2, *pb1, k1, p1, pb1, k2; rep from * to end.
Row 3 P2, *kb1, p1, k1, kb1, p2; rep from * to end.
Row 4 K2, *pb1, p1, k1, pb1, k2; rep from * to end.
Repeat these 4 rows.

THROW

Using 4.00mm needles and Col 1, cast on 86 sts.
Work in Stitch Patt, work until piece measures 1.5metres (or length desired). Cast off.
Make 3 pieces as set using Col 1, and 2 pieces using Col 2.

MAKING UP

Lay pieces horizontally side by side and sew together using Edge to Edge stitch.
Fringe Take 4, 30cm lengths of yarn and fold in half. Insert crochet hook through the edge of rug and pull the folded end through forming a loop. Reach the hook down and draw all the ends through the loop. Pull the ends down to tighten the knot against the edge. Make 74 tassles placed evenly across each end of throw to form fringe (ie 14 tassles on each section end).

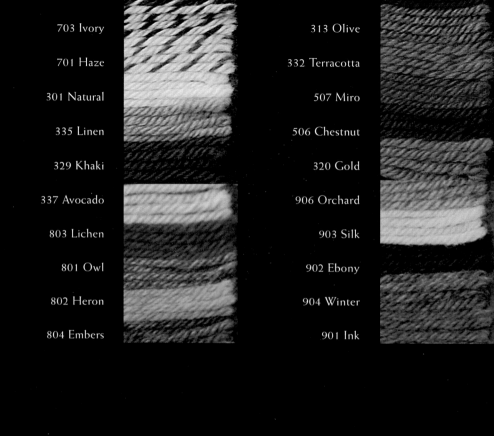

703 Ivory

701 Haze

301 Natural

335 Linen

329 Khaki

337 Avocado

803 Lichen

801 Owl

802 Heron

804 Embers

313 Olive

332 Terracotta

507 Miro

506 Chestnut

320 Gold

906 Orchard

903 Silk

902 Ebony

904 Winter

901 Ink

How to care for your pure wool knitwear

Investment Knitting

With care the Jo Sharp garment you create this year will become a trusted favourite in the years to come. Spun from premium grade long fibre fleece, Jo Sharp yarn knits into a hard-wearing item of clothing that is beautifully warm and soft. It is not surprising that Jo's wool performs so well when you consider it has survived all the elements while still on the sheep's back. Pure wool is practical, long-lasting and natural. A Jo Sharp wool garment will stand up to harsh outdoor conditions whilst keeping its softness and good looks throughout years of wear.

Wool knitwear requires care and attention when it is washed, however it does not soil easily and requires maintenance less frequently than other fibres.

Not machine wash treated

Jo Sharp Hand Knitting Yarn has a natural crimp and elasticity which makes it satisfying to knit with. Its waxy outer coating of tiny overlapping scales, (rather like roof shingles) repels liquids and particles of dust or dirt. Wool contains millions of tiny pockets of air which act as natural thermal insulators. Unfortunately, machine wash treatment puts an artificial resin coating on wool fibres, effectively gluing them together and damaging natural thermal characteristics. This treatment also gives wool yarn an un-natural shiny appearance. For these reasons, Jo Sharp chose not to machine wash treat her yarn.

Less Pilling

Inferior short fibres (which can cause pilling and itching) are removed during processing of Jo Sharp yarn. This treatment improves the yarn's natural softness and wash and wear performance. With care, your quality Jo Sharp garment will improve with age and wear.

What causes wool knitwear to shrink?

Nature designed wool fibres to be a protective coating for sheep in all weather. The unique outer scale structure of the wool fibre resists soiling, but is also the reason why wool shrinks when not cared for properly. With severe agitation or tumble drying, the scales on the fibre lock together causing the garment to reduce in size and become thick and fluffy (felted). If you carefully follow the washing instructions on the inside of the Jo Sharp yarn label and right, you should not encounter any problems with shrinkage.

Hand Washing

For the best result, turn garment inside out and gently hand wash in lukewarm water, using a wool detergent. Rinse thoroughly in lukewarm water. Rinse again in cold water.

Drying

To remove excess moisture after washing, roll garment inside a large towel and gently squeeze or, alternatively, spin dry inside a pillow case. Never tumble dry. Place garment on a flat surface in the shade to dry, coaxing it back into shape whilst damp. Drying flat is recommended.

Do not dry directly in front of an open or artificial fire.

Machine washing

If care is taken, a Jo Sharp wool garment may be successfully machine washed. Turn the garment inside out and place inside a sealed pillow slip (sew pillow closed or use a special casing for wool washing that zips closed). Use a wool detergent and a gentle cycle with a medium spin and lukewarm water. Any severe agitation may shrink your garment. Dry as above.

Dry cleaning

Generally is not recommended as residual dry cleaning chemicals tend to harden wool fabric.

Combing

When our extra long fibre yarn is processed, most of the short fibres are removed. If, in the first few weeks of wear, a few remaining short fibres shed, causing a small amount of pilling, these pills should be combed from your garment using an EEZY fabric comb, available from craft and knitting stores.

Yarn Specification

Jo Sharp 8ply DK Pure Wool Hand Knitting Yarn is made from extra fine and soft 100% Merino/Border Leicester fleece.

(DK is the USA and UK equivalent of Australian 8 ply)

One Ball of yarn is 50g (1 3/4 oz)

and approx. 98 Mtrs (107 yards) in length.

Tension/Gauge: 22.5 sts and 30 rows, measured over 10cm of Stocking Stitch and using 4.00 mm (UK 8) (USA 6) needles.

JO SHARP

Hand Knitting Collection Stockists

AUSTRALIA
Head Office & Mail Order Enquiries
JO SHARP HAND KNITTING YARN
PO Box 357 Albany
Western Australia 6330
Telephone +61 08 9842 2250
Facsimile +61 08 9842 2260
email - josharp@fullcomp.com.au

Australian Retail Stores Enquiries
Coats Spencer Crafts
Private Bag 15, Mulgrave North
Victoria Australia 3171
Telephone 03 9561 2288
Facsimile 03 9561 2298
Toll Free 1800 641 277

New South Wales

Champion Textiles	Newtown	02 9519 6677
Cherry Hill	Pennant Hills	02 9484 0212
Clairheath	Penrith	04 732 2201
Greta's Handcraft Centre	Lindfield	02 9416 2489
Hand to Hand Crafts	Newcastle	04 929 7255
Jimana Crafts	Lindfield	02 9416 2489
Knit It	Eastwood	02 9874 1358
Lady Ann	Woy Woy	02 4342 2249
Grace Bros.	North Ryde	02 9887 0122
Sue's Baby Beanies	Annandale	02 9560 7498
Yarn'n'Things	Winston Hills	02 9560 7498

Australian Capital Territory

Shearing Shed	Kingston	02 6295 0061
Stitch 'n' Time	Mawson	02 6286 4378

Queensland

Miller & Coates	Ascot	07 3268 3955

Tasmania

Knitters of Australia	Moonah	03 6229 6052
Needle & Thread	Devonport	03 6424 6920
The Needlewoman	Hobart	03 6234 3966
The Spinning Wheel	Hobart	03 6234 1711
Wool Place	Glenorchy	03 6272 3313

South Australia

Midway Fabrics	Port Lincoln	08 8682 2641
Highgate Needle Nook	Highgate	08 8271 4670
Pee Jays	Ingle Farm	08 8264 8515

Victoria

Audrey's Wool Shop	Altona	03 9938 9293
Bayswater Wool Centre	Bayswater	03 9729 6915
Healesville Art & Craft	Healesville	03 5962 2266
Knight's Habby	Kyabram	03 5852 2862
Knit & Purl Warehouse	Dandenong	03 9793 3530

Knitters of Australia	Hampton	03 9533 1233
Knitters of Australia	Surrey Hills	03 9836 9614
Marra Emporium	Reservoir	03 9469 4400
Mooroolbark Craft & Habby	Mooroolbark	03 9726 7291
Mornington Wool Centre	Mornington	03 5975 4247
Myer	Melbourne	03 9661 1111
Pingvin	Maffra	03 5147 2135
Purl Plain & Petit Point	Portland	03 5523 6044
Simply Wool	Warrandyte	03 9844 1264
Singer Sewing Centre	Colac	03 5231 3252
Sunbury Wool Centre	Sunbury	03 9744 4520
The Stitcher	Essendon	03 9379 9790
Warrnambool Wool & Uniforms	Warrnambool	03 5562 9599
Wool Village	Mulgrave	03 9560 5869
Wool Shed Crafts	Watsonia	03 9432 3544

Western Australia

Anne's Machine Knitting Shop	Rockingham	08 9527 1606
Crossway's Wool & Fabrics	Subiaco	08 9381 4286
email: woolshop.com.au		
Hedy's Wool Corner	Albany	08 9841 5148
Myer	Perth	08 9221 3444

NEW ZEALAND
Mail Order Enquiries
Knit-A-Holics Unlimited
PO Box 45083
Epuni Railway
Lower Hutt, NZ
Telephone 04 567 4085
Facsimile 04 567 4094
email: knitting@xtra.co.nz

Creative Fashion Centres	Lower Hutt	04 232 8088
	Tawa	07 838 3868
	Hamilton	07 838 3868
Knit World	Auckland	09 837 6111
	Palmerston North	06 356 8974
	New Plymouth	06 758 3171
	Christchurch	03 379 2300
	Hastings	06 878 0090
	Tauranga	07 577 0797
	Dunedin	03 477 0400
	Wellington	04 385 1918
Knit'n'Save	Lower Hutt	04 567 7688
	Levin	06 367 9700
	Paraparaumu	04 298 8756

CANADA
Wholesale Enquiries
Estelle Designs
Units 65/67 2220 Midland Ave.
Scarborough, Ontario M1P 3E6
Telephone 416 298 9922
Facsimile 416 298 2429

Canadian Retail Stores

Alberta	Wool Revival	Edmonton	403 471 2749
British Columbia	Boutique de Laine	Victoria	250 592 9616
	House of Wool	Prince George	604 562 2803
Manitoba	Ram Wools	Winnipeg	204 942 2797
	The Sheep Boutique	Winnipeg	204 786 8887
Ontario	Christina Tandberg Knits	London	519 672 4088
	Elizabeth's Wool Shop	Kitchener	519 744 1881
	Imagiknit 2000	Orillia	705 689 8676
	Knit or Knot	Aurora	905 713 1818
	London Yarns & Machines	London	519 474 0403
	Muskoka Yarn Connection	Bracebridge	705 645 5819
	Needles and Knits	Aurora	905 713 2066
	Passionknit Ltd	Toronto	416 322 0688
	Romni Wool	Toronto	416 703 0202
	The Celtic Fox	Toronto	416 487 8177
	The Celtic Fox	North York	416 944 3351
	The Needle Emporium	Ancaster	905 648 1994
	The Yarn Tree	Streetsville	905 821 3170
	Village Yarns	Toronto	416 232 2361
	Wool-Tyme	Carlingwood	613 798 0869
	Wool-Tyme	Nepean	613 225 WOOL
Saskatchewan	The Wool Emporium	Saskatoon	306 374 7848

U.S.A.
Wholesale Enquiries
Classic Elite Yarns
12 Perkins Street Lowell, MA 01854
Telephone 978 453 2837
Facsimile 978 452 3085

U.S.A. Retail Stores

Arizona	Red Rock Knit Shop	Sedona	520-204-1505	www.theshoppingsite.com/redrockneedlepoint/
	Purl's II	Tucson	520-797-8118	
California	Navarro River Knits	Ft. Bragg	707-964-9665	
	BB's Knits	Santa Barbara	805-569-0531	
	Yarn Collection	Mill Valley	415-383-9276	
	In Sheep's Clothing	Davis	530-759-9276	www.insheepsclothing.com
	Knitting in LaJolla	LaJolla	619-456-4612	
	The Black Sheep	Encinitas	760-436-9973	
	Velona's	Anaheim Hills	714-974-1570	
	L'Atelier	Redondo Beach	310-540-4440	
	L'Atelier	Santa Monica	310-394-4664	
	In Stitches	Santa Barbara	805-962-9343	
	Uncommon Threads	Los Altos	650-941-1815	

	Greenwich Yarns	San Francisco	415-567-2535	www.citysearch.com/sfo/greenwichyarn
	Filati Fine Yarns	Danville	925-820-6614	
	Fabrications	Grass Valley	530-272-4412	www.fabrications-gv.com
Connecticut	Wool Connection	Avon	800-933-9665	www.woolconnection.com
	The Yarn Barn	Woodbridge	203-389-5117	
	Hook & Needles	Westport	800-960-4404	www.hook-n-needle.com
Delaware	Not Just Needlepoint	Wilmington	302-426-1244	
Idaho	Isabel's	Ketchum	208-725-0408	
	Ewe K Knits Ltd/			
	House of Needlecraft	CoeurD'Alene	888-775-5648	www.ewekknit.com
Illinois	Mosaic Yarn Studio	Des Plaines	847-390-1013	www.mosaicyarnstudio.com
	The Village Knit Whiz	Glenview	847-998-9772	
	Basket of Stitches	Palatine	847-991-5515	
	Fine Line	St. Charles	630-584-9443	
	Barkim Ltd.	Chicago	888-548-2211	www.barkim.com
	The Weaving Workshop	Chicago	773-929-5776	
	Nancy's Knitworks	Springfield	800-676-9813	
Indiana	Sheep's Clothing Supply	Valparaiso	219-462-4300	
Louisiana	The Purple Giraffe	Lafayette	318-984-7323	
Massachusettes	Knitting Treasures	Plymouth	508-747-2500	
	Barehill Studios	Harvard	978-456-8669	
	KnitWits	Brookfield	1-877-877-knit (5648)	www.knitwitts.com
	Northampton Wools	Northampton	413-586-4331	
	Colorful Stitches	Lenox	800-413-6111	www.colorful-stitches.com
	I'm in Stitches	Newburyport	978-465-2929	
	Woolcott and Co.	Cambridge	617-547-2837	
	Wild & Woolly Studio	Lexington Ctr.	781-861-7717	
	Snow Goose	Milton	617-698-1190	
	Creative Warehouse	Needham	781-444-9341	
	Ladybug Knitting Shop	Dennis	508-385-2662	www.ladybugknitting.com
Maryland	Woolworks	Baltimore	410-337-9030	
	Yarn Garden of Annapolis	Annapolis	410-224-2033	
Maine	Stitchery Square	Camden	207-236-9773	www.stitching.com/stitcherysquare
Michigan	Yarn Quest	Traverse City	616-929-4277	
	Right Off the Sheep	Birmingham	248-646-7595	
	Madeline's	Grand Haven	616-844-2011	
	The Wool & The Floss	Grosse Pointe	313-882-9110	
	Threadbender	Grand Rapids	888-531-6642	www.threadbender.com
	Knitting Room	Birmingham	248-540-3623	
Missouri	Thread Peddler	Springfield	417-886-5404	
	Hearthstone Knits	St. Louis	314-849-9276	
	Lynn's Stitchin Tyme	Marshfield	417-859-4494	
Minnesota	Linden Hills Yarns	Minneapolis	612-929-1255	
	A Sheepy Yarn Shoppe	White Bear Lake	800-480-5462	
	Three Kittens Yarns Shop	St. Paul	612-457-4969	
	Zandy's Yarn Etc.	Burnsville	612-890-3087	
	Skeins	Minnetonka	612-939-4166	
	Needlework Unlimited	Minneapolis	612-925-2454	
North Carolina	Great Yarns	Raleigh	919-832-3599	
Nebraska	Personal Threads Boutique	Omaha	402-391-7733	www.personalthreads.com
New Hampshire	Keepsake Yarnworks	Centre Harbor	603-253-4725	
	The Elegant Ewe	Concord	603-226-0066	
	Yarn Express	Center Ossipee	603-539-4397	
	Charlotte's Web	Exeter	888-244-6460	

New Jersey	The Knitting Gallery	Colts Neck	732-294-9376	
	Simply Knit	Lambertville	609-397-7101	
	Knitters Workshop	Garwood	908-789-1333	
	Accents on Knits	Morristown	973-829-9944	
New Mexico	Village Wools	Albuquerque	800-766-4553	www.villagewools.com
	The Needle's Eye	Santa Fe	505-982-0706	
New York	The Knitting Corner	Huntington	516-549-9109	
	Happiknits	Commack	516-462-5558	
	The Knitting Place, Inc.	Port Washington	516-487-2595	
	Elegant Needles	Skaneateles	315-685-9276	
	The Yarn Connection	New York	212-684-5099	www.nytoday.com/yarnconnection
	Lee's Yarn Center	Bedford Hills	914-244-3400	
	Heartmade (mail order only)	Brooklyn	800-898-4290	
	Patternworks	Poughkeepsie	800-438-5464	www.patternworks.com
	Village Yarn Shop	Rochester	716-454-6064	
Ohio	Wolfe Fibre Arts	Columbus	614-487-9980	
	Fifth Stitch	Defiance	419-782-0991	
Oklahoma	Sealed with a Kiss	Guthrie	405-282-8649	www.swakknit.com
	Mary Jane's	Oklahoma City	405-848-0233	
	Needlework Creations	Tulsa	918-742-0448	
Oregon	Woodland Woolworks	Yamhill	503-662-3641	
	Fiber Nook & Crannys	Corvallis	541-754-8637	
	Northwest Peddlers	Eugene	800-764-9276	www.nwpeddlers.com
	Websters	Ashland	541-482-9801	
Pennsylvania	Mannings Creative	E. Berlin	800-233-7166	www.the-mannings.com
	Oh Susanna Yarns	Lancaster	717-393-5146	
	Ewe & I	Bryn Mawr	601-520-0440	
	A Garden of Yarn	Chaddsford	610-459-5599	www.yarngarden.com
	Wool Gathering	Kennett Square	610-444-8236	www.woolgathering.com
Rhode Island	Fabric Place	Warwick	401-823-5400	www.fabricplace.com
	A Stitch Above	Providence	800-949-5648	
Tennesee	Angel Hair Yarns	Nashville	615-269-8833	www.angelhairyarn.com
	Genuine Purl Too	Chattanooga	423-267-7335	
	Knit & Purl	Knoxville	423-690-9983	
Texas	Needleart	Spring	281-288-0585	
	Woolie Ewe	Plano	972-424-3163	
	Turrentines	Houston	713-661-9411	
	Yarn Barn	San Antonio	210-826-3679	
	Donna's Yarn Barn	Austin	512-452-2681	
Utah	Needlepoint Joint	Ogden	801-394-4355	www.needlepointjoint.com
Virginia	Hunt Country Yarns	Middleburg	540-687-5129	
	Aylin's Woolgatherer	Falls Church	703-573-1900	
	Wooly Knits	Mclean	703-448-9665	www.woolyknits.com
	Old Town Needlecrafts	Manassas	703-330-1846	
	Knitting Basket Ltd	Richmond	804-282-2909	
	Orchardside Yarn Shop	Raphine	540-348-5220	
	The Knitting Corner, Inc.	Virginia Beach	757-420-7547	
	On Pins & Needles	Toano	757-566-0621	
Washington	The Weaving Works	Seattle	888-524-1221	
	Tricoter	Seattle	206-328-6505	
Wisconsin	Jane's Knitting Hutch	Appleton	920-954-9001	www.angelfire.com/biz2/yarnshop/index.html
	Easy Stitchin' Needleart, Inc.	Sister Bay	920-854-2840	
	Ruhama's Yarn & Needlepoint	Milwaukee	414-332-2660	
	Herrschners Inc.	Stevens Point	1-800-713-1239	

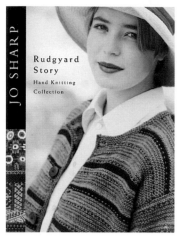

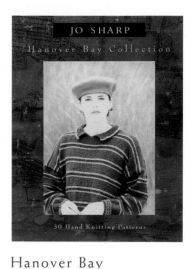

Rudgyard Story Collection

With 112 full colour pages and 33 designs, this soft cover book offers projects for knitters of all skill levels, including beginners.

West Cape Howe Collection

This 40 page soft cover book contains 25 designs, each illustrated in full colour with projects suitable for knitters of all skill levels. If you have always wanted to design your own multi-colour sweater, you will find a designers blank sweater graph to get you started.

Hanover Bay Collection

With 48 pages and 30 designs, all illustrated in full colour, this soft cover book contains projects to suit knitters of all skill levels.

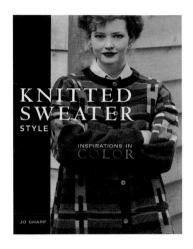

Individual Pattern Leaflet Collection
This collection of Jo Sharp favourites is containted in 22 individual pattern leaflets. The leaflets can be found only in craft or knitting stores which stock the Jo Sharp yarn collection on pages 102 - 105.

Knitted Sweater Style
This classic hard cover book is published by The Taunton Press and contains 42 designs for hand knitting.
It incorporates most of the Jo Sharp individual pattern leaflet collection featured at left.

Shade Card
Jo Sharp works exclusively with her own shade collection as illustrated on page 100.
The yarn sample card is available by contacting a Jo Sharp yarn stockist as listed on pages 102 - 105.

The Durango Button Company
1021 C.R. 126
Hesperus, CO. 81326
U.S.A.
Contact the above address to obtain buttons for the following designs in this book; Emporium/Version 2, Ariel/Version 1 and Boheme/Version 2 Quote button code as per pattern.

For information about where to obtain these publications, see the Jo Sharp stockist listing on page 102 - 105

JO SHARP

Jo Sharp lives in Albany,
a large country town on
the south coast of Western
Australia with her husband
and two children.
Albany is known for its
magnificent coastline,
annual whale visits and
wineries.
Jo began her career in
textiles in 1986 designing
colourful Intarsia knitwear
for fashion boutiques
throughout Australia.
She now works exclusively
with her own unique
collection of yarns creating
designs for hand knitters.